Earth's Water

by Lorrie Oestreicher

PEARSON

Scott
Foresman

DK

The Water of Life

All living things need water to survive. Plants, animals, fish, insects, birds, and human beings all depend on water to stay alive.

Think about food, shelter, clothing, and water. Which is the most important? If you answered water, you are right. We need the others also, but without water we could live for only a few days.

Many of Earth's living things spend their entire lives in the water. You know about animals such as fish and clams and other sea creatures. But there are also lots of living things in the water that are difficult to see. For instance, a living thing called a paramecium lives in ponds and lakes. A paramecium is much too small to see without a microscope!

A magnified paramecium

All Living Things Need Water

About two-thirds of your body is made up of water. It helps your body's parts work correctly.

We must drink plenty of water because our bodies lose a lot of it through sweat. We sweat water to keep our bodies at the right temperature.

Tears in your eyes wash out dust. Saliva in your mouth helps to digest food. Blood, which is mostly water, carries oxygen and nutrients through your body. The water in your blood also carries away waste from your organs.

Running makes us sweat.

This land is watered so that crops can grow.

How We Use Water

Farmers who grow lots of food use huge amounts of water to raise their crops. More than half of the world's fresh water is used for growing food. Farmers bring water to their fields from rivers, lakes, reservoirs, and wells. That allows them to grow crops in places that get very little rain.

People have learned to use water in many ways. Huge ships can move easily in water. Because of that, people can move goods from place to place all over the world.

When people learned to use the power of water, many things changed. Dams were built to block rivers. They help control flooding. Dams also help make electricity. People all over the world use electricity from dams to heat and light up their homes.

Salt Water versus Fresh Water

Almost three-fourths of Earth is covered by the salt water of the oceans. People use salt water for transportation and fishing. Salt water cannot be used for drinking, bathing, or cooking. It cannot be given to animals. It also does great harm to land-based plants, so it cannot be used to water crops.

Almost $\frac{3}{4}$ of the world's surface is covered by water.

A small part of the world's water is fresh water.

Most of the world's water is salt water.

Only a small part of Earth's water is fresh water. Fresh water is found in ice, snow, rivers, lakes, streams, and in the ground. About two-thirds of that fresh water is frozen in glaciers and ice caps at the North and South Poles. That leaves little fresh water for people, plants, and animals to live on!

Lake

River

The fresh water in streams and rivers is always flowing. Gravity makes a lot of fresh water sink beneath Earth's surface. Fresh water that is below the surface is called **groundwater.** By digging wells, people bring groundwater up to the surface.

When a river, lake, or stream overflows or floods, wetlands are created. **Wetlands** are marshy, soggy areas that soak up the extra water from the land. They help control flooding. Many birds and animals are adapted to live in wetlands.

Well

Wetlands

Water, Ice, and Steam

When you put water into a tray and set it in the freezer, its temperature drops. When it reaches 32 degrees Fahrenheit, the water freezes and becomes a solid. Snow and hail are also solid forms of water.

When water is heated, it evaporates, becoming **water vapor.** The process is called **evaporation.** Evaporation causes water to change from liquid to gas without boiling. The surface water on lakes and oceans is constantly evaporating into the air due to heating from the Sun.

Freezing point in degrees Fahrenheit and degrees Celsius

Water vapor rises into the air

Water vapor is invisible. But we can feel it on humid days. On humid days we feel "sticky" because our sweat doesn't evaporate as well.

At night when the Sun goes down, the air cools. Water vapor may turn back into a liquid at that time. This process is called **condensation.** Dew is a type of condensation. It helps plants grow. Clouds and fog are also formed by condensation.

Dew on a flower

Water on the Move

Rain clouds

Earth's water is used over and over again. It travels between the air, the land, and the oceans in an endless circle called the **water cycle.**

When raindrops hit the ground, different things may happen. Puddles form on surfaces such as sidewalks. Raindrops that have fallen on sidewalks often evaporate.

Raindrops that have fallen on earth often seep downward through rocks and soil. They may reach groundwater. By doing so, they help refill the underground water supply.

If raindrops don't evaporate or soak into the soil, they may run downhill into a stream, river, or lake. Then the drops may be carried to the ocean.

Clouds form as the water vapor cools.

Water vapor rises from the ocean.

No matter how much water evaporates into the air, it always falls back to Earth in some form of precipitation. **Precipitation** may fall as rain, sleet, snow, or hail. If the air is cold enough, raindrops freeze into hail. Snow is made of tiny ice crystals in clouds. Whichever way water returns to Earth, the water cycle starts again.

Clouds rise and cool, and rain falls.

Water vapor rises from the land.

13

Making Water Clean

Water contains substances we cannot see. Many of them are good for us. But water can also contain things that are dangerous for us to drink. Pollution, germs, and chemicals in water can make us sick. Because of that we must add and remove things from our water before we drink it.

Cities and towns treat fresh water before it comes into our homes and businesses. Water is piped in from wells, rivers, streams, lakes, and reservoirs.

A city needs a lot of clean water.

On its way to the city, the water is cleaned by filters. The first filter catches large objects. Another filter made of sand and gravel takes out any impurities that are left. Then air is bubbled through the water to make it taste fresh. Certain safe chemicals are added to get rid of germs and make the water safe to drink.

Water filtering

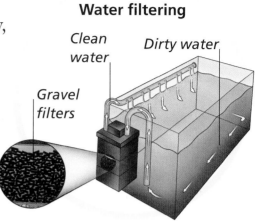

Clean water

Dirty water

Gravel filters

Glossary

condensation the process that turns a gas into a liquid

evaporation the process in which a liquid changes into a gas

groundwater water that flows or seeps downward and collects beneath the soil

precipitation all water that falls to Earth from clouds in the form of rain, sleet, snow, or hail

water cycle the movement of water from Earth's surface into the air and back again

water vapor water that has risen into the air as an invisible gas

wetlands lowland areas, such as marshes or swamps, that are flooded with water